Photographs

to think about

by

Mary Clover Moran

Dedicated

to

My husband,

Patrick Stephen Moran,
who helped make this book possible.

Copyright: 2018

Author's Note

The pictures in this book were taken over many years. I have been very fortunate to have visited many places and seen many things. I also had the opportunity to bring my camera with me wherever I went and I loved taking pictures to remind me of the things I have seen. I hope my readers will enjoy my work and be inspired to capture their journeys with a camera through life.

Skyscraper in New York

This picture is a puzzle.
See if you can figure
what is up and
what is down.

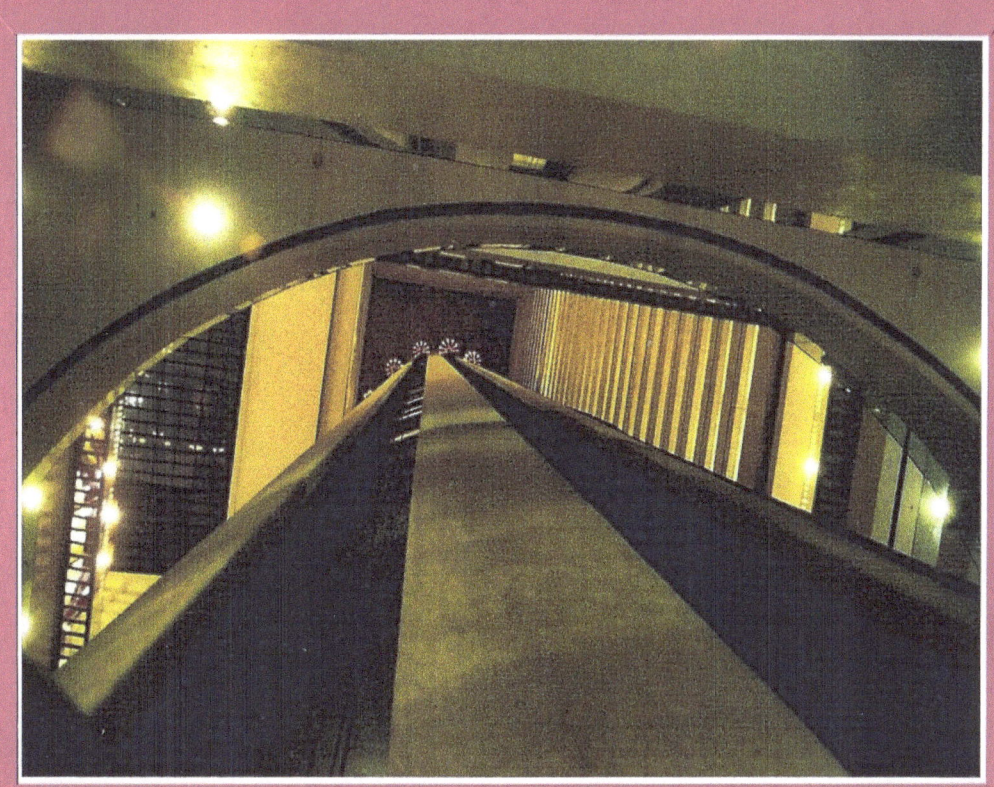

The Puzzle

What do you see in this picture?
Sometimes, I think I am seeing
an ear, and sometimes it looks
like a face. It's very strange,
coming out of the concrete.

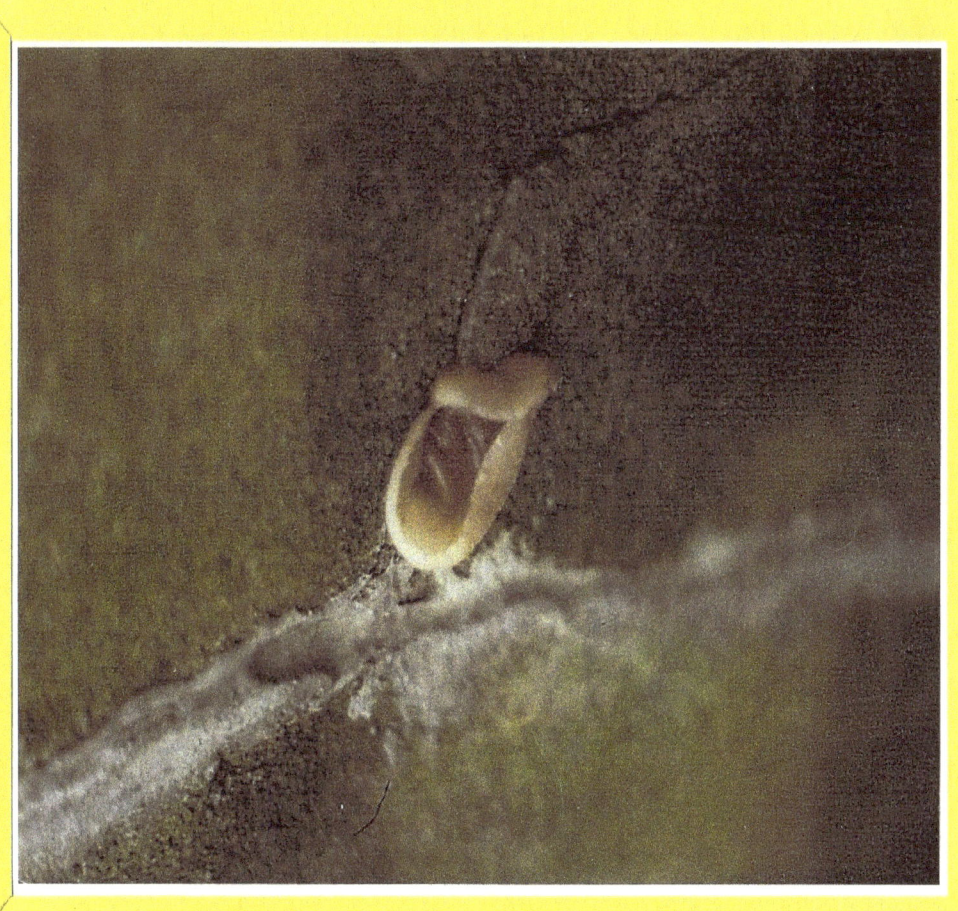

The Canopy

Have you ever sat in a park under the trees and looked straight up? See how beautiful it is up there.

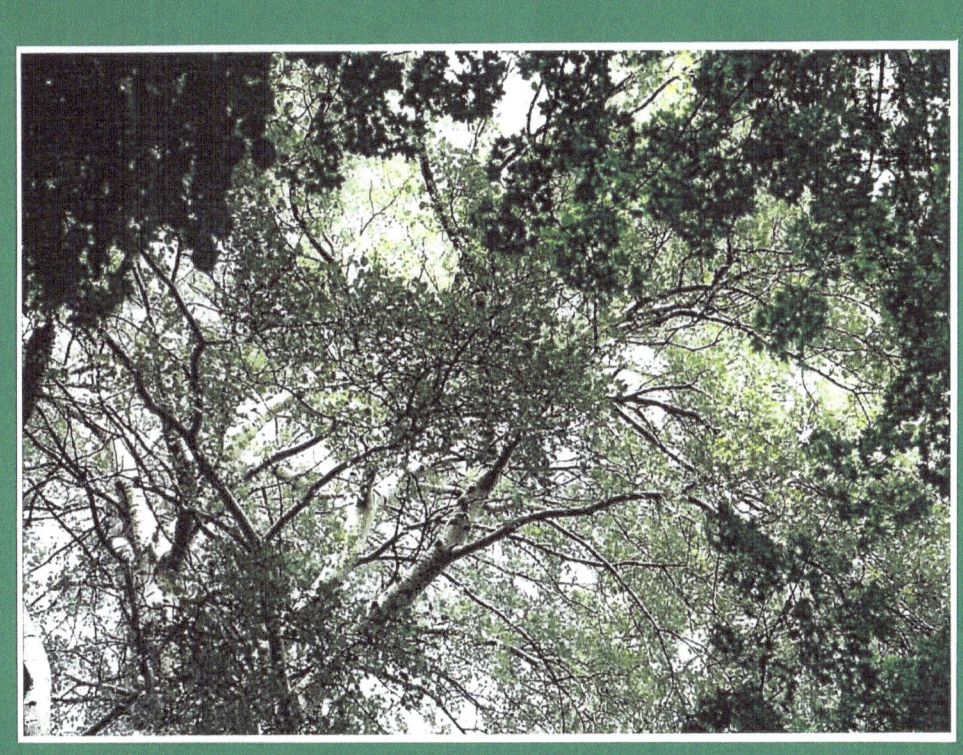

Whitewing

Would you believe you are
looking at a crow? Well,
you are. He lived in our yard
for a whole year.

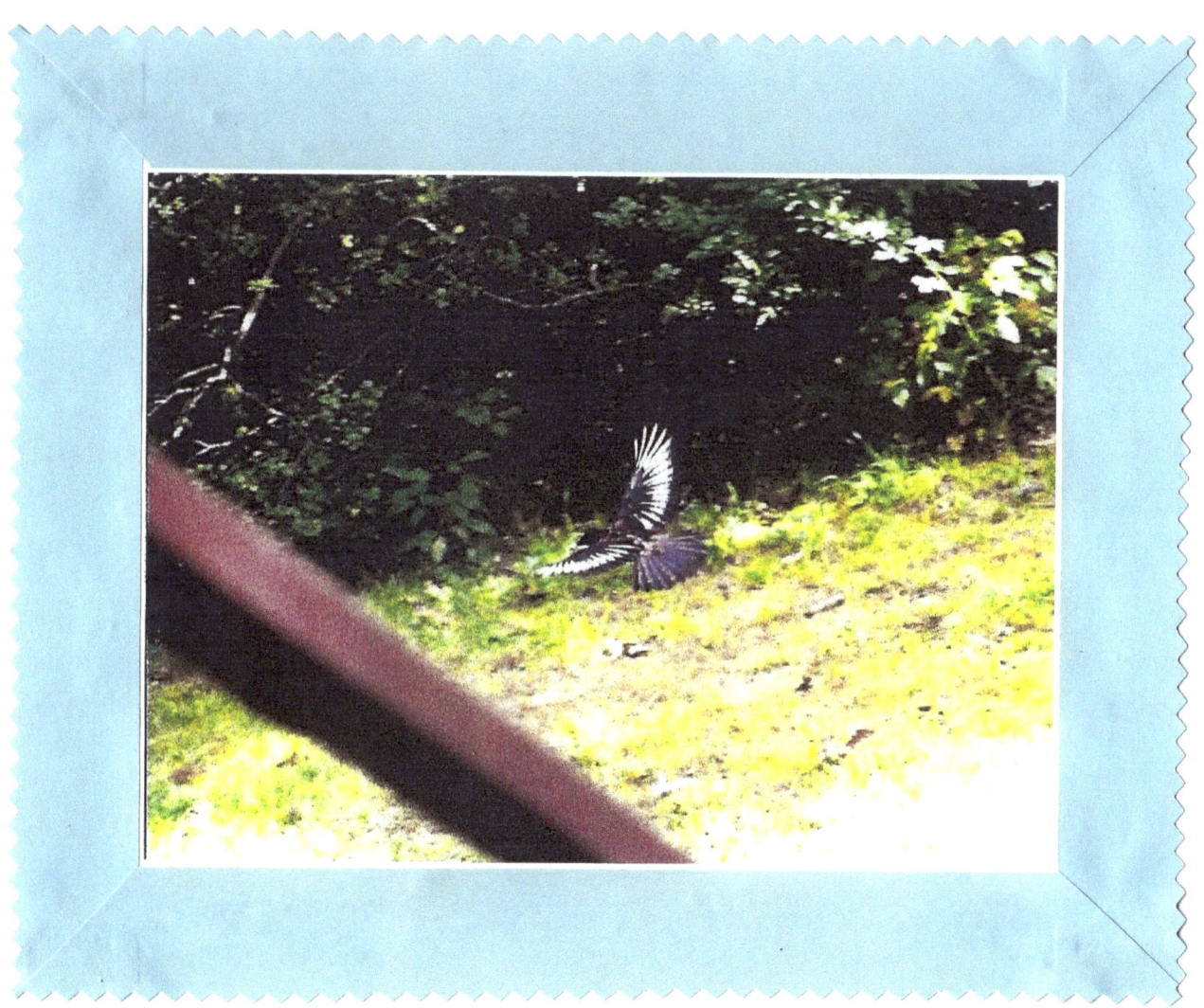

The Squirrel

Is this squirrel really
angry or just very hungry?
What do you think?

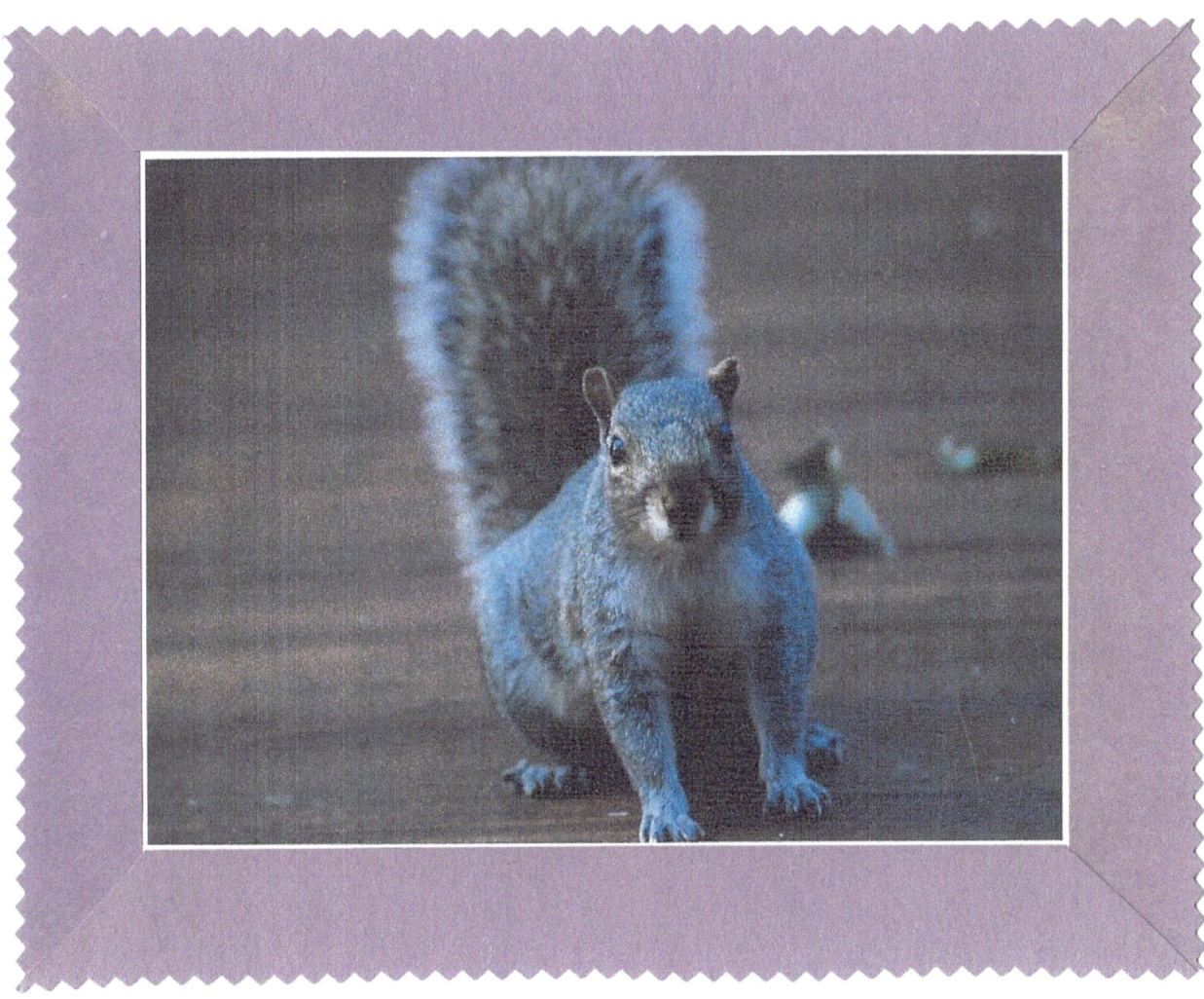

Alone

What would you do if you came to swim in a swim meet and you were the only swimmer there? The timers are all ready and waiting. Do you think you can win this one?

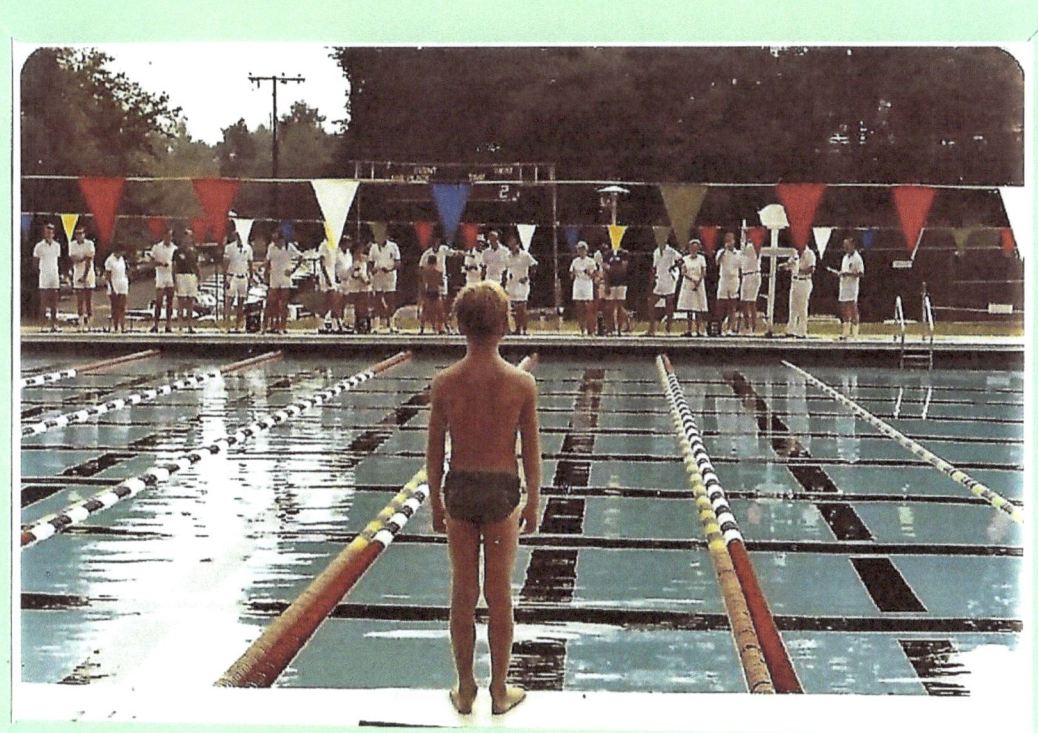

Mohini

What color are tigers supposed to be? Are you surprised that this one is white? I liked him so much that I named my favorite cat after him, Mohini.

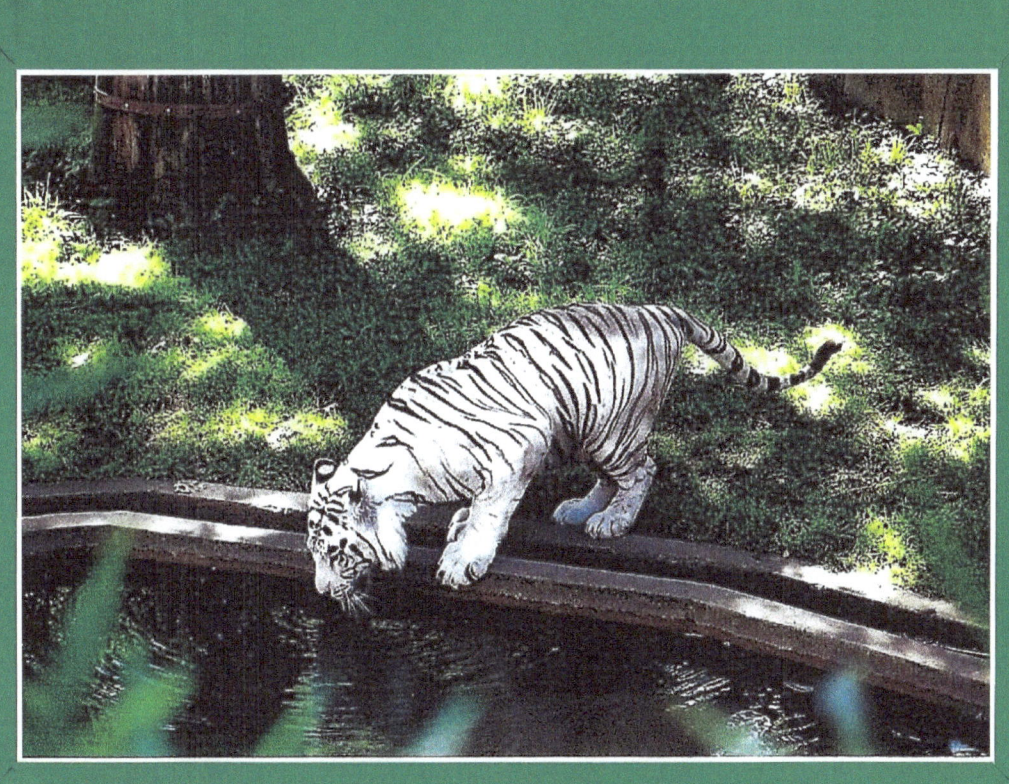

View From Above

How did I get this picture?
Where do you think I might be?
Can you imagine how many
people are below me?

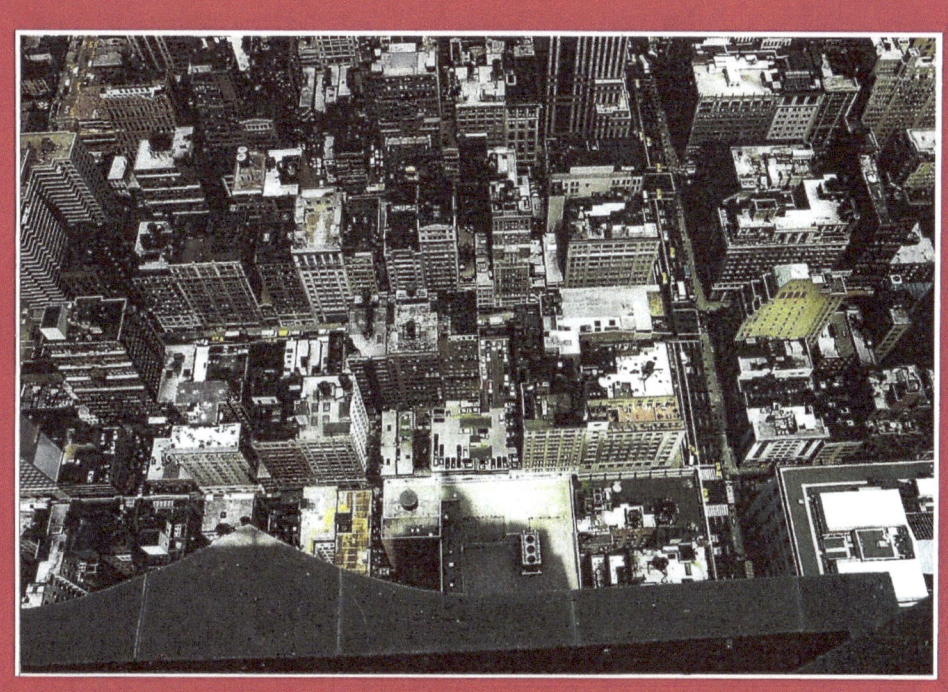

My Beautiful Visitor

How can something so tiny be so beautiful? This hummingbird is a very special gift from God.

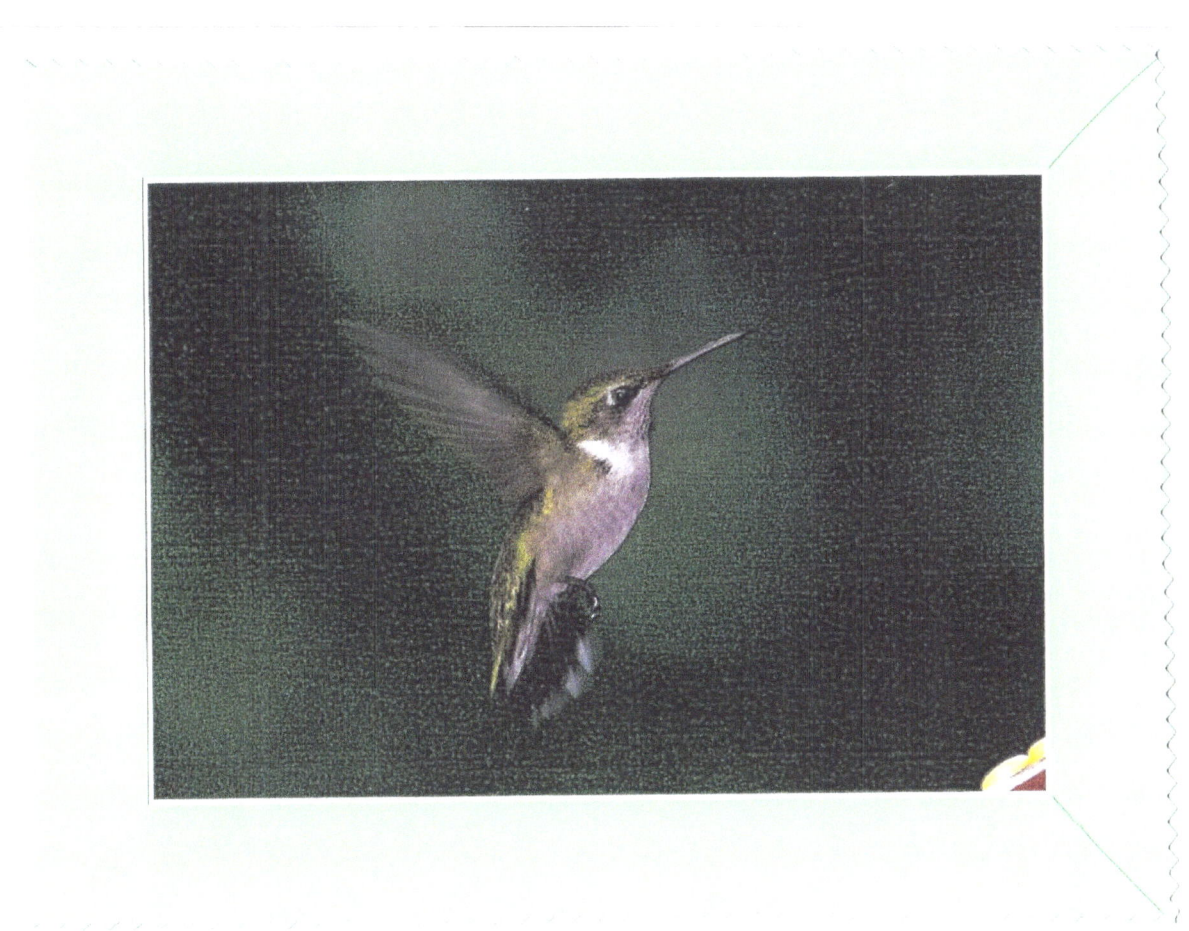

The Tomato

Have you ever thought of your food as something beautiful, a work of art? This tomato is God's work of art **and** it tastes good, too.

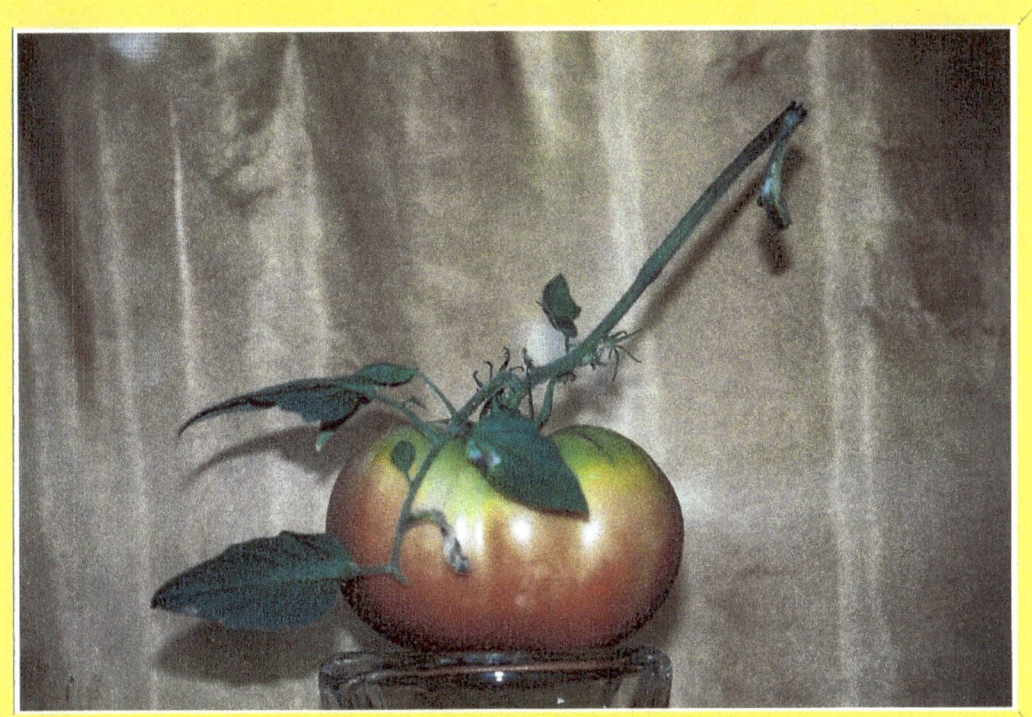

A Beautiful Bunny

If he stays very still,
do you think the fox
will see him? I hope not.

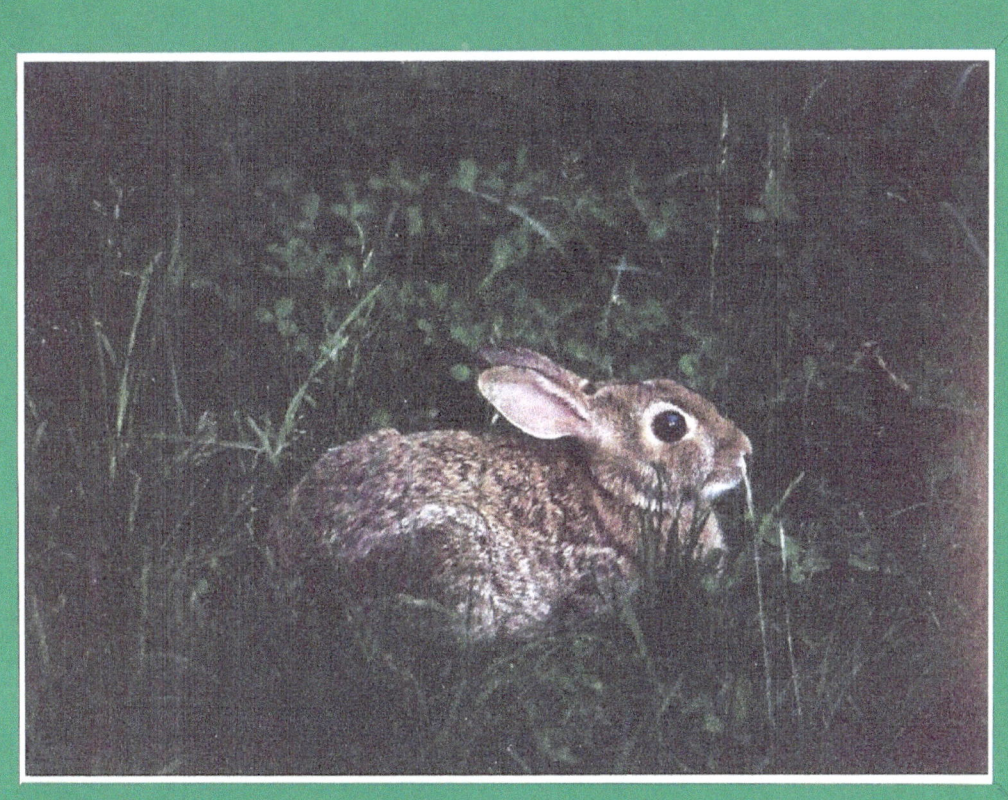

Nailsworth

Where do you think this might be? Would you call it a city or something else? Could it be a village somewhere? It looks very hilly to me. What do you think about it?

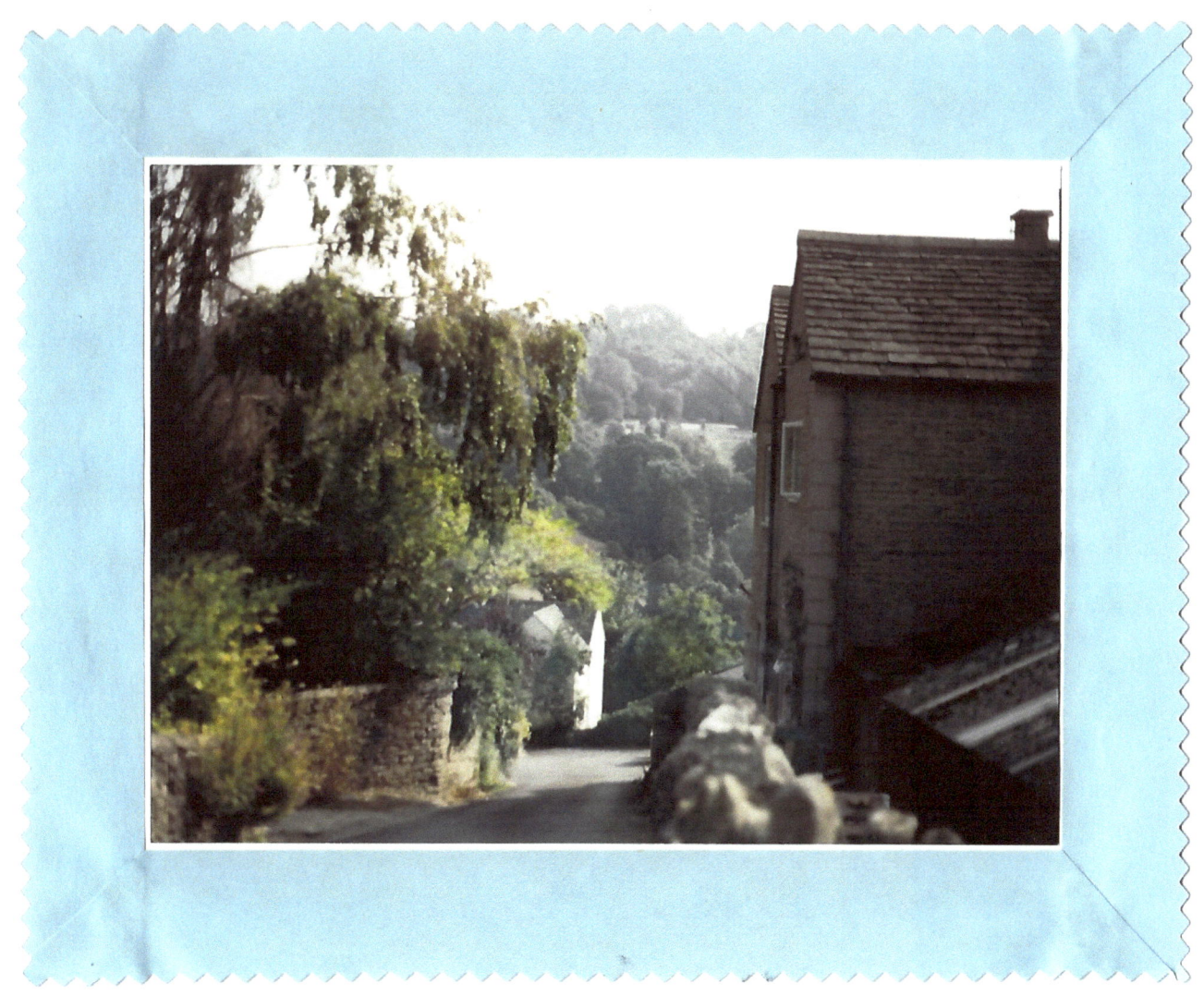

Snowball

How many squirrels
like this have you seen?
Not many I think.

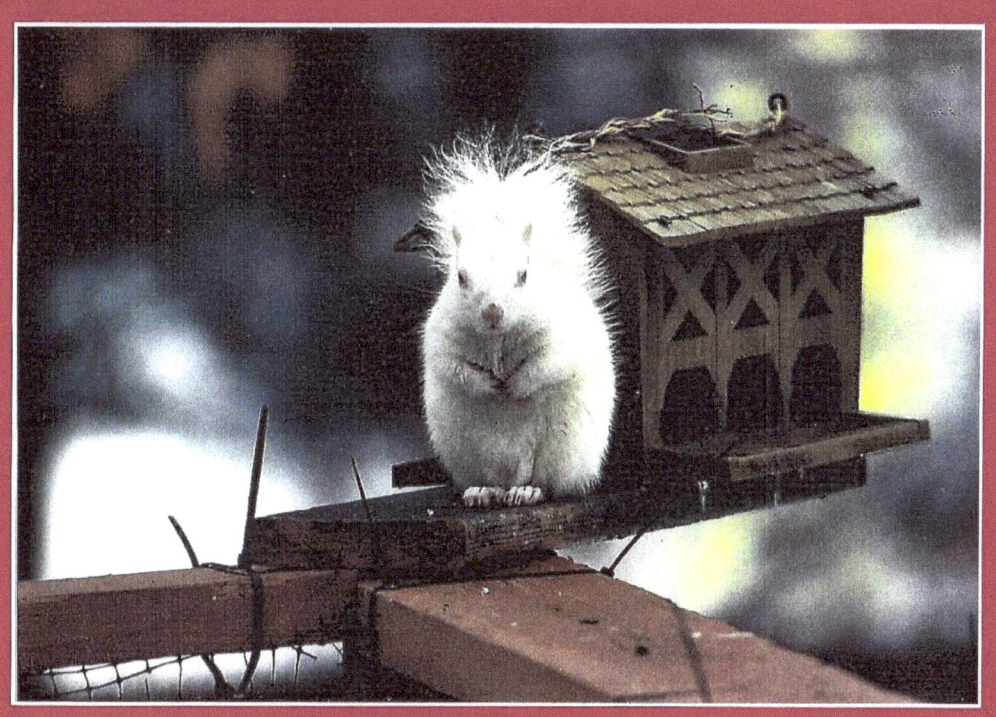

Trees in the Mist

Is there something
coming through the mist?
Look carefully and maybe,
you might see something.

The Cliffs

Does this look like a place
you would like to slide
down, all the way to the sea?

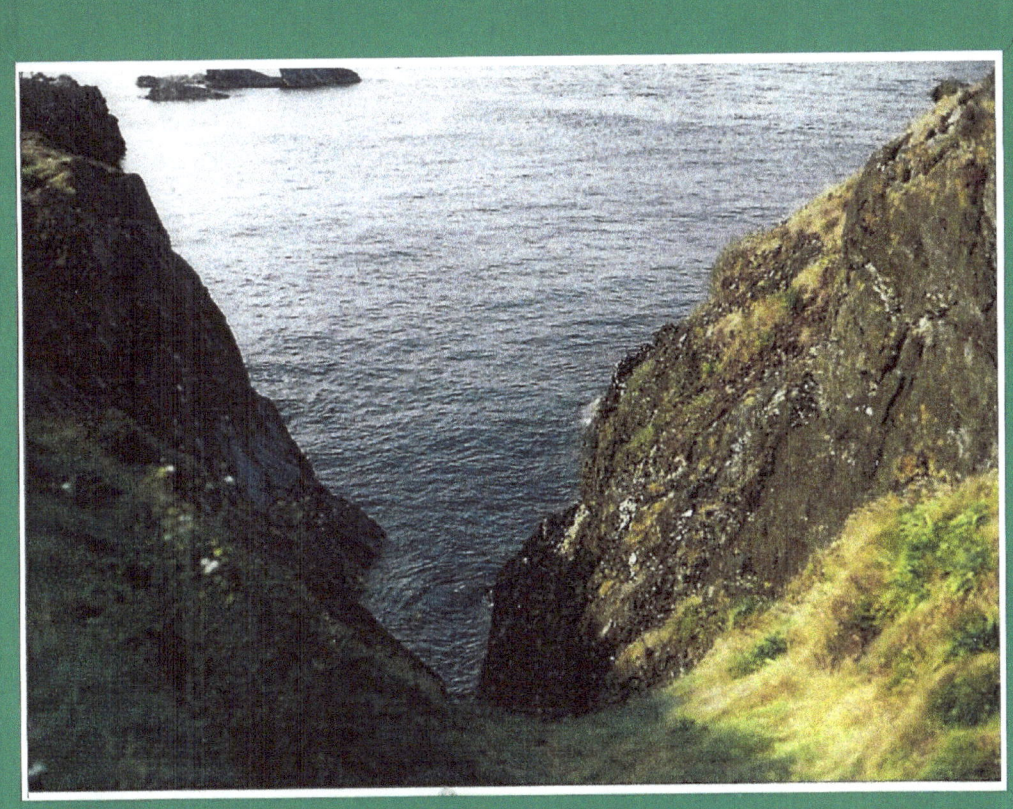

Truck Delivery

What can be done on an island
with no bridge and no airport?
This is the only way to get things
there, by barge, of course!

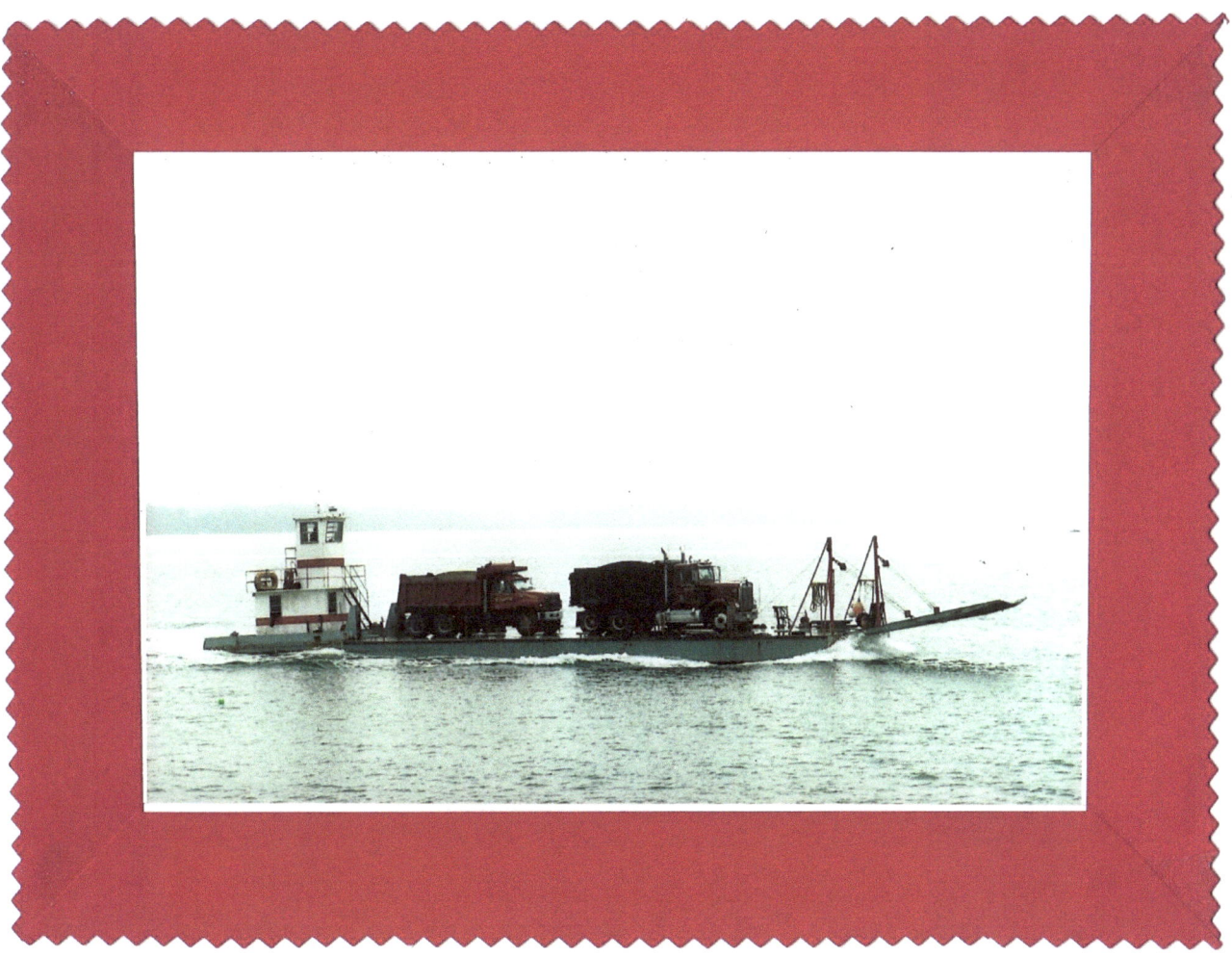

My Fox

Do you think of foxes as
mean and wild creatures?
This one just wants to
enjoy the sun.

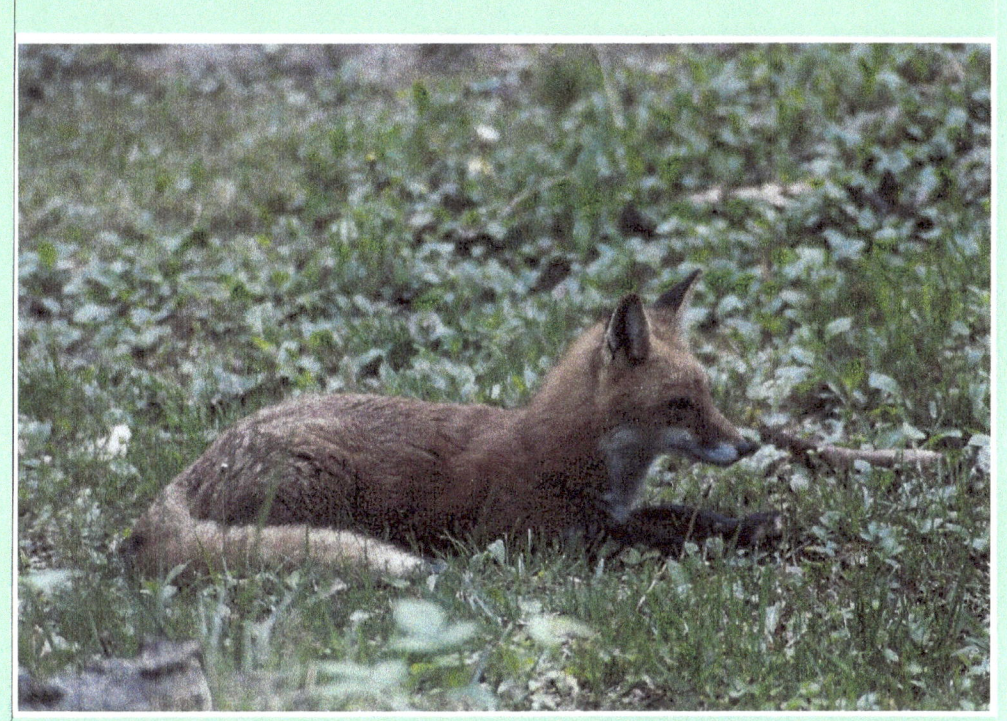

The Hawk

Can you imagine a hawk
just sitting on a fence and
letting me take his picture?

Well, he did.

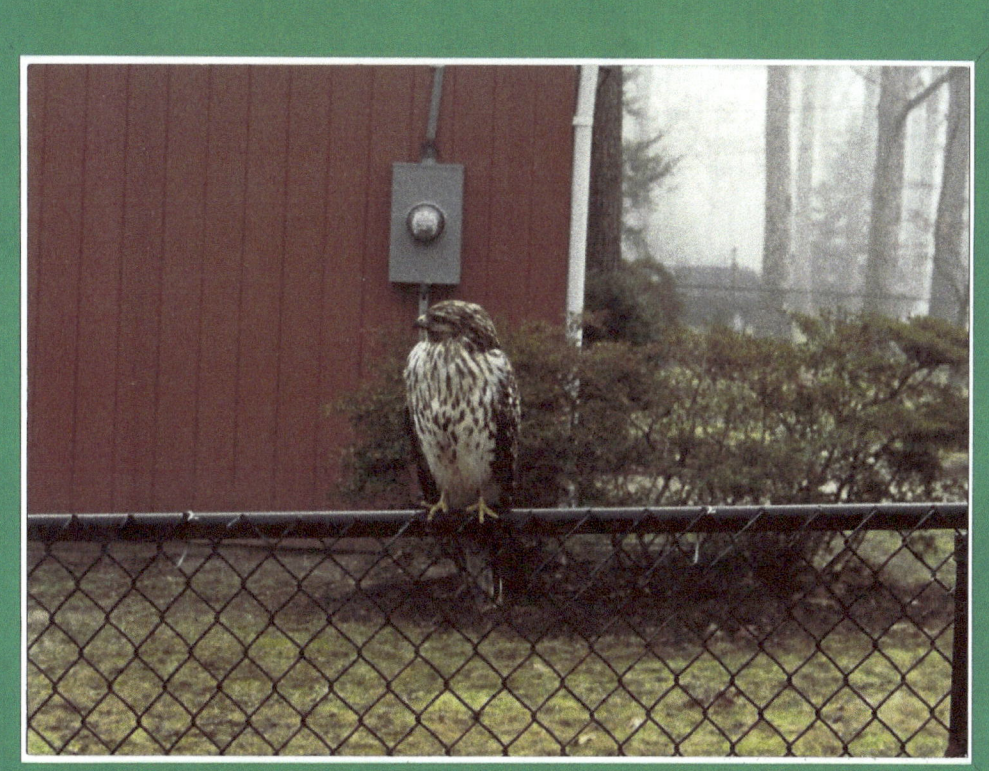

Mystery

Is the moon being held
up by the tree branches?
You can never be sure.

The Black Roofs

What kind of buildings might these be? Can you guess? What gives you a hint about them? If you were to go to Ireland, you might get to visit them.

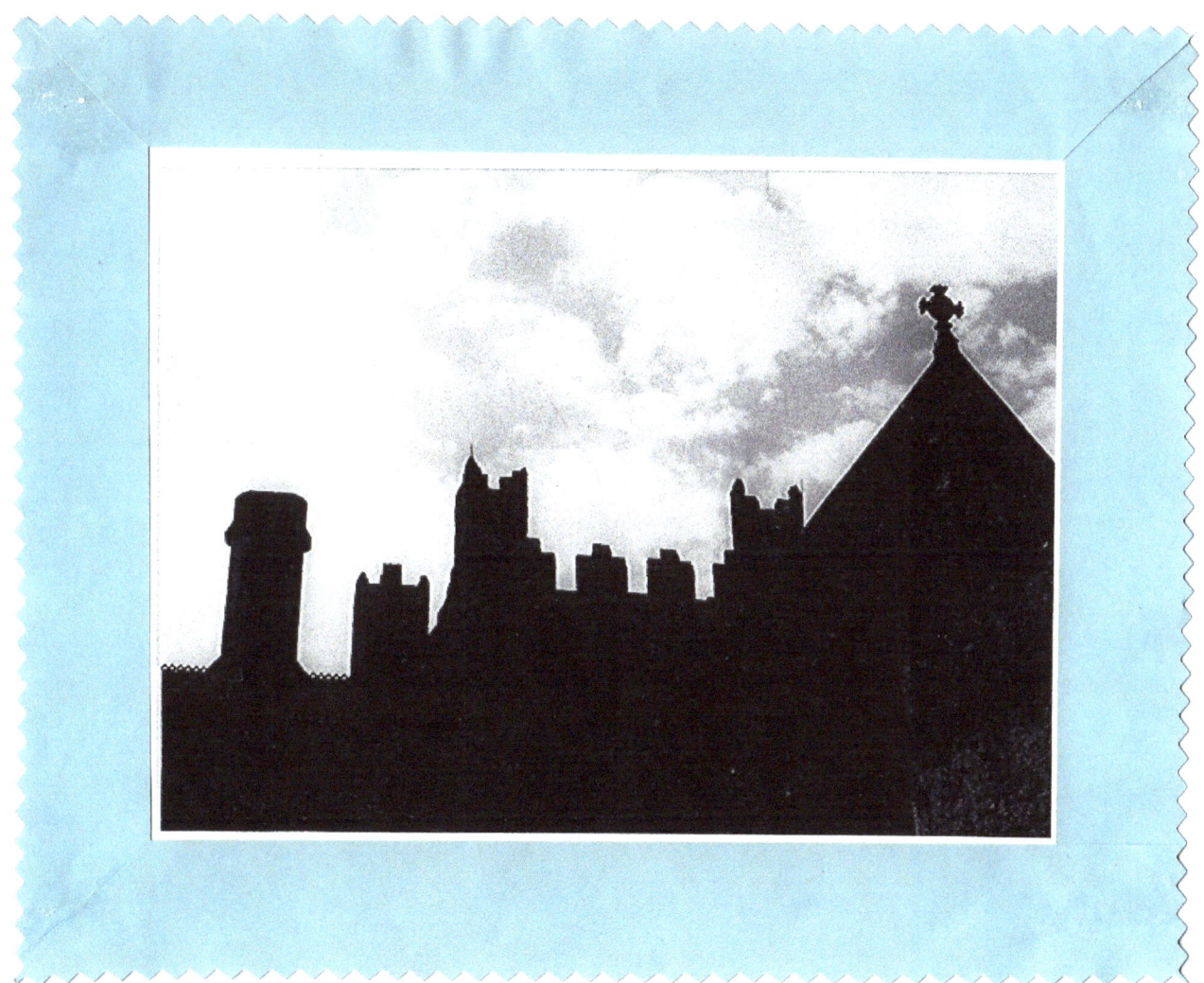

Saint Pope John Paul II

When I took this picture, I never dreamed I would have a picture of a saint. When Pope John Paul II came to Baltimore, we had a chance to see him. He rode his Pope mobile around the stadium and stopped right in front of us. So many people wanted to take his picture and there he was, right in front of me and I had my camera ready.

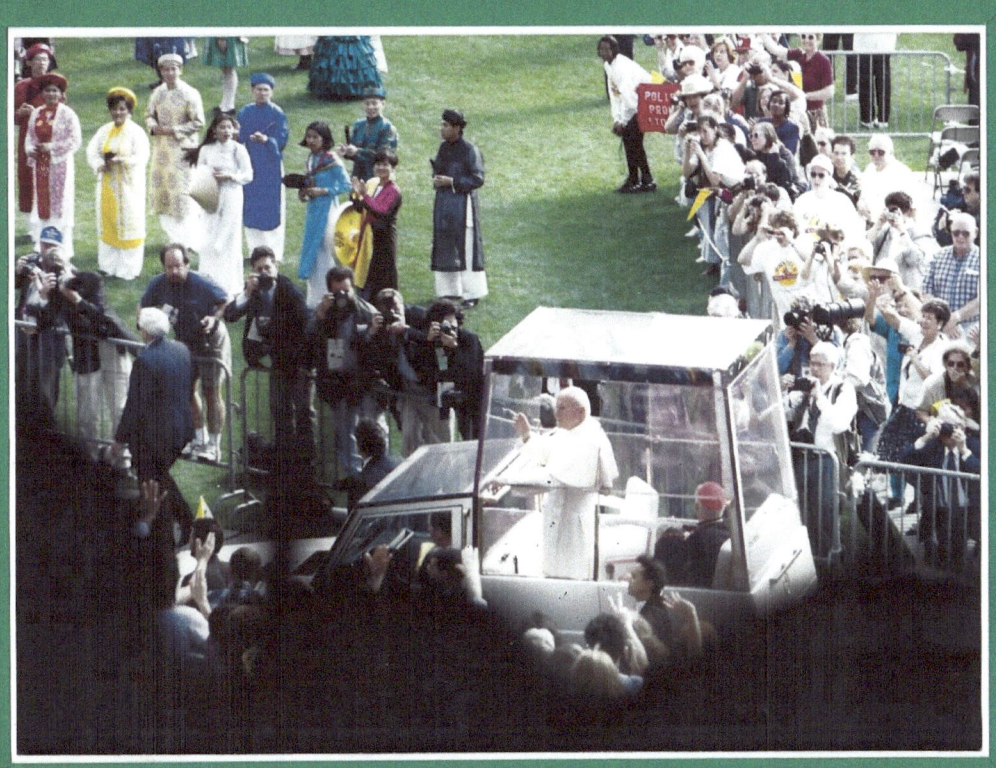

The City Before

When I took this picture on a trip to New York City in July, 2001, I never could have imagined that in 2 short months, those 2 beautiful, tall buildings would be gone and the New York City skyline would be changed forever.

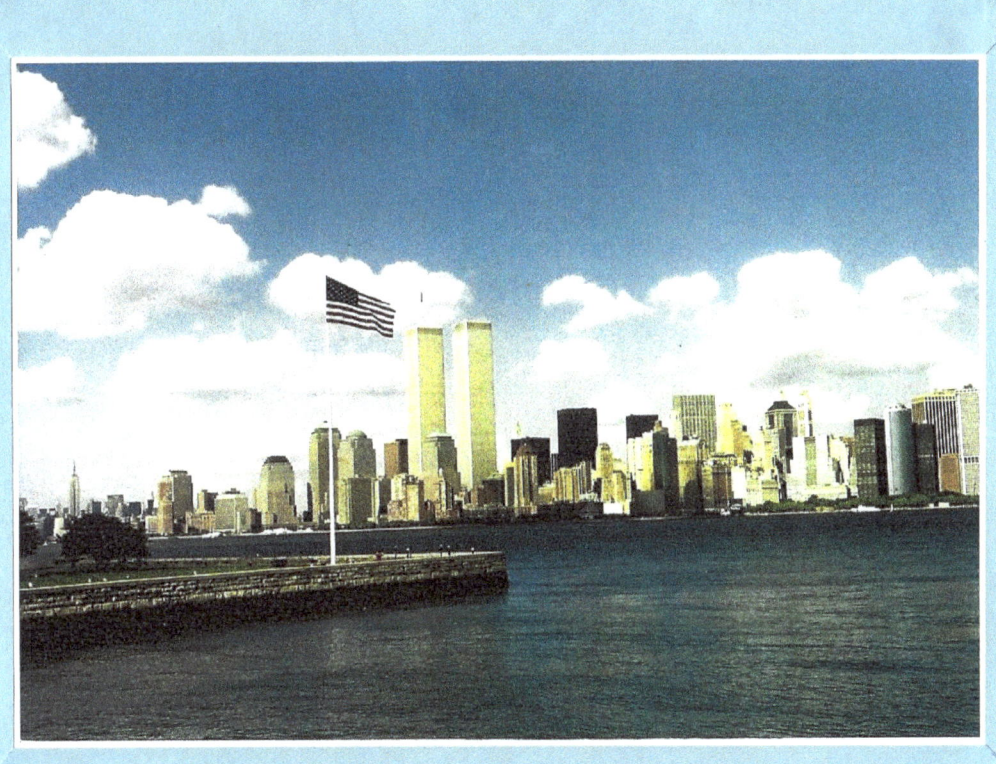

Togetherness

Two little girls, working together to water the grass. Wouldn't it be **wonderful** if all the people in the world could work together like these little ones, watering the whole world and making it **blossom with love**?

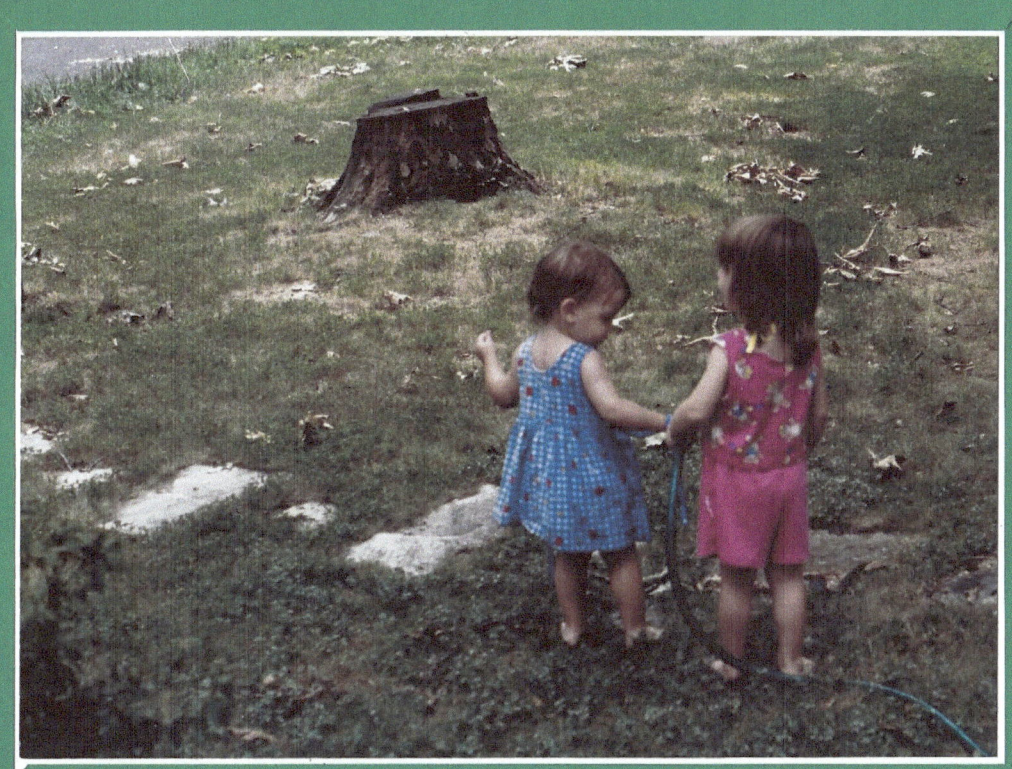

Dear Reader,

   I hope you have enjoyed sharing my adventures.

   Now go and make your own memories to share with others.

Books by Mary Clover Moran

Available at Amazon.Com

"Breakfast at the Birdfeeder" — A picture story of squirrels not birds. (2012)

"Digby's Rescue" — The story of a duck who found himself in unfamiliar territory and how he found help. (2012)

"Mommy. Where's Our Baby? - An interactive, consolation story for a young child who has lost a baby brother or sister. (2015)

"Surprises for Mary" — A story about Our Blessed Mother Mary and her responses to each event in her life as the Mother of Jesus. (2011)

"Thoughts for Young People" — A story for grade school children, to help them understand the teachings of the Catholic Church regarding The Mass and Miracles. (2013)

"The Owl in the Closet" — A Fairy Tale of Friendship and how the owl found a friend forever. (2010)

www.ingramcontent.com/pod-product-compliance
Lightning Source LLC
Chambersburg PA
CBHW051215220526
45473CB00003B/1038